Bloom

Guided Rosary Journal
for Women

Maria Alberto

Bloom
Copyright © 2022 by Maria Alberto

All rights reserved. No part of this publication may be reproduced, distributed, or transmitted in any form or by any means, including photocopying, recording, or other electronic or mechanical methods, without the prior written permission of the author, except in the case of brief quotations embodied in critical reviews and certain other non-commercial uses permitted by copyright law.

Tellwell Talent
www.tellwell.ca

ISBN
978-0-2288-8689-1 (Paperback)

Table of Contents

Author's Note v

Joyful Mysteries

The Annunciation 2
The Visitation 3
The Nativity 4
The Presentation 5
Finding in the Temple 6

Luminous Mysteries

The Baptism of Jesus 8
Wedding at Cana 9
Proclamation of the Kingdom of God 10
The Transfiguration 11
Institution of the Eucharist 12

Sorrowful Mysteries

The Agony in the Garden 14
Scourging at the Pillar 15
The Crowning with Thorns 16
The Carrying of the Cross 17
Crucifixion and Death of our Lord 18

Glorious Mysteries

The Resurrection 20
The Ascension 21
The Descent of the Holy Spirit 22
The Assumption of Mary 23
The Coronation of Our Lady 24

Further Resources 25

Author's Note

This journal has been developed for you, just as you are, in this season of life. You may be riding a high, you may be enduring a low. This is for you. Just as there are flowers in each season, this is designed to help you bloom wherever you are at... whether it is your spring or your winter.

You can use this journal as you pray a Rosary, or as a stand alone resource to reflect on the Mysteries. You may like to keep it as a personal prayer tool, or use it as a discussion starter within a trusted group. In any case, I hope the prompts lead to greater self-awareness, draw you closer to Jesus, and support you in living 'to the full'.

May Mother Mary intercede for you, and may you receive a renewed sense of God working in your life.

Maria

For Dennis, Julian and Adreana.

Joyful Mysteries

The Annunciation
The Angel Gabriel appeared to the Virgin Mary (Lk 1:26-38)

The angel Gabriel was sent by God to a town called Nazareth, to a virgin betrothed to a man named Joseph. The virgin's name was Mary. Gabriel went in and said to her, "Rejoice, you who enjoy God's favor! The Lord is with you. Look! You are to conceive in your womb and bear a son, and you must name him Jesus. He will be great, and will be called the Son of the Most High. He will reign over the house of Jacob forever, and of his kingdom there will be no end." "How will this be," Mary asked, "since I am a virgin?" The angel answered, "The Holy Spirit will come upon you and the child to be born will be holy; he will be called Son of God. And now, your relative Elizabeth in her old age has also conceived a son; and this is the sixth month for her who was said to be barren. For nothing will be impossible with God." Mary said, "You see before you the Lord's servant, let it happen to me as you have said."

"Nothing will be impossible for God". Imagine if we lived with full confidence that God can not only do all things, but can (and will) resolve all problems. Imagine what our everyday experience would be if we surrendered everything to God with the mentality that He will 'sort it out'. This is surely how Mary had the courage to respond with a 'yes' that has resounded in to eternity. Spend some time reflecting on what you need to entrust to God:

....
....
....
....
....
....
....
....
....
....

Lord, you can do all things!

The Visitation

Mary visits her cousin Elizabeth (Lk 1:39-42)

Mary set out and went in haste to a town in Judah. She went into Zechariah's house and greeted her cousin Elizabeth, who had miraculously conceived in her old age. Now it happened that as soon as Elizabeth heard Mary's greeting, the child leapt in her womb and Elizabeth was filled with the Holy Spirit. She gave a loud cry and said, "Of all women you are the most blessed, and blessed is the fruit of your womb."

Mary went to support Elizabeth in her time of need, despite her own pregnancy. Those months were likely filled with back rubs, cooking meals and praying for one another. This Mystery challenges us to care for others, even when we have needs of our own. Like Mary, this can be (and often is) through simple everyday acts. Consider how you might 'love your neighbor' in this way and write your reflections below:

....
....
....
....
....
....
....
....
....
....
....
....
....

I want to serve like Mary.

The Nativity
Jesus was born, God Incarnate (Lk 2:6-14)

Now it happened that, while they were there, the time came for her to have her child. She gave birth to a son, her first-born. She wrapped him in swaddling clothes and laid him in a manger because there was no room for them in the living-space. In that region there were shepherds out in the field, keeping watch over their flock by night. And an angel of the Lord appeared to them, and the glory of the Lord shone around them. The angel said to them, "Be not afraid; for behold, I bring you good news of a great joy which will come to all the people; for to you is born this day in the city of David a Saviour, who is Christ the Lord. And this will be a sign for you: you will find a babe wrapped in swaddling cloths and lying in a manger." And suddenly there was with the angel a multitude of the heavenly host praising God and saying, "Glory to God in the highest, and on earth peace among men with whom he is pleased!"

The Son of God, King of Kings, was born in a humble stable. There was mess, probably stench, and yet it was the setting for the Incarnation. This Mystery reminds us that God does not want an edited, manicured version of our lives. He wants to be born within the stables of our hearts, amidst our mess and chaos. Spend some time reflecting on areas that you may consider your 'mess' and note down your thoughts:

....
....
....
....
....
....
....
....
....
....

Lord, come in to my mess.

The Presentation

Jesus was taken to the Temple (Lk 2:25-32)

Now there was a man in Jerusalem whose name was Simeon. This man was righteous and devout, awaiting the consolation of Israel, and the Holy Spirit was upon him. It had been revealed to him by the Holy Spirit that he should not see death before he had seen the Messiah of the Lord. Moved by the Spirit, he came into the temple; and when the parents brought in the child Jesus to perform the custom of the law in regard to him, he took him into his arms and blessed God, saying: "Now, Master, you may let your servant go in peace, according to your word, for my eyes have seen your salvation, which you prepared in sight of all the peoples, a light for revelation to the Gentiles, and glory for your people Israel."

Simeon trusted in God's promises, despite not knowing the timing of their fulfillment. He waited in hopeful anticipation with patience and faith. This Mystery challenges each of us to trust in God's plan and holy purpose for our life, even when it feels like nothing is happening. Reflect on things in your life that you don't fully understand, but want to entrust to God:

....
....
....
....
....
....
....
....
....
....
....
....

Lord, I trust in your promises for my life.

Finding in the Temple
Jesus was found in the Temple (Lk 2:41-50)

Each year Jesus' parents went to Jerusalem for the feast of Passover, and when he was 12 years old, they went up according to festival custom. After they had completed its days, as they were returning, the boy Jesus remained behind in Jerusalem, but his parents did not know it. Thinking that he was in the caravan, they journeyed for a day and looked for him among their relatives and acquaintances. But not finding him, they returned to Jerusalem to look for him. After three days they found him in the temple, sitting in the midst of the teachers, listening to them and asking them questions. All who heard him were astounded at his understanding and his answers. When his parents saw him, they were astonished, and his mother said to him, "Son, why have you done this to us? Your father and I have been looking for you with great anxiety." And he said to them, "Why were you looking for me? Did you not know that I must be in my Father's house?" But they did not understand what he said to them.

Imagine how stressed Mary and Joseph were as they desperately searched for their son. Three days is a long time for anyone to be missing, let alone a child! Yet, Jesus challenges their anxiety. This Mystery invites us to trust in Jesus even (and most especially) when we are worried. Use this space to write about something that is creating anxiety or stress in your life which you would like to offer to the Lord:

....
....
....
....
....
....
....
....
....
....

Jesus, I offer up my worries.

Luminous Mysteries

The Baptism of Jesus
Jesus is baptized and declared the Son of God (Mt 3:13-17)

> Then Jesus came from Galilee to John at the Jordan to be baptized by him. John tried to prevent him, saying, "I need to be baptized by you, and yet you are coming to me?" Jesus said to him in reply, "Allow it now, for it is fitting for us to fulfill all righteousness." Then he allowed him. After Jesus was baptized, he came up from the water and behold, the heavens were opened and he saw the Spirit of God descending like a dove coming upon him. And a voice came from the heavens, saying, "This is my beloved Son, with whom I am well pleased."

In this Mystery, John is so very relatable. Despite his virtues and courageous ministry, he doubts his worthiness to participate in God's work. How often have we felt unworthy to serve God? Perhaps our doubt is rooted in the wounds of our past, perhaps it stems from the falsehoods of sin. Whatever the case, it is easy to question why God would choose us to do His work. But, He has! Reflect on your gifts and talents and how God is calling you to use them:

....
....
....
....
....
....
....
....
....
....
....
....

Lord, use me for your glory.

Wedding at Cana
Jesus performs his first public miracle, turning water in to wine (Jn 2:3, 7-11)

When the wine ran short, the mother of Jesus said to him, "They have no wine." Jesus said to her, "Woman, how does your concern affect me? My hour has not yet come." His mother said to the servers, "Do whatever he tells you." Now there were six stone water jars there for Jewish ceremonial washings, each holding twenty to thirty gallons. Jesus told them, "Fill the jars with water." So they filled them to the brim. Then he told them, "Draw some out now and take it to the headwaiter." So they took it. And when the headwaiter tasted the water that had become wine, without knowing where it came from (although the servers who had drawn the water knew), the headwaiter called the bridegroom and said to him, "Everyone serves good wine first, and then when people have drunk freely, an inferior one; but you have kept the good wine until now." Jesus did this as the beginning of his signs in Cana in Galilee and so revealed his glory, and his disciples began to believe in him.

Jesus said "It is not yet my time" but still did what Mary asked of him. His change of heart was probably because of a soft spot he has for his mum (like so many people do). It isn't a long stretch to think that this unique relationship between Jesus and Mary has continued beyond Jesus' time on earth... she was his mother, after all. This Mystery is a beautiful reminder that Mary can take our intentions to Jesus and, perhaps, give him a little nudge to respond. Write any intentions you would like Mary to take to Jesus:

....
....
....
....
....
....
....
....

Mary, take these petitions to your son.

Proclamation of the Kingdom of God

Jesus proclaimed the Kingdom of God (Mk 1:14-15; 2:3-12)

Unable to get near Jesus because of the crowd, four men opened up the roof above him. After they had broken through, they let down the mat on which the paralytic was lying. When Jesus saw their faith, he said to the paralytic, "Child, your sins are forgiven." Now some of the scribes were sitting there asking themselves, "Why does this man speak that way? He is blaspheming. Who but God alone can forgive sins?" Jesus immediately knew in his mind what they were thinking to themselves, so he said, "Why are you thinking such things in your hearts? Which is easier, to say to the paralytic, 'Your sins are forgiven,' or to say, 'Rise, pick up your mat and walk'? But that you may know that the Son of Man has authority to forgive sins on earth"— he said to the paralytic, "I say to you, rise, pick up your mat, and go home." He rose, picked up his mat at once, and went away in the sight of everyone. They were all astounded and glorified God, saying, "We have never seen anything like this."

Consider how the paralytic completely relied on his friends to take him to Jesus. It was their faith and efforts which led to his miraculous healing. This is a reminder of how important friends are on our faith journey. Our paralysis may not necessarily be physical, but could come in a mental or spiritual form. What in your life requires 'miraculous healing'? Who in your life would 'break through the roof' and lay you before Jesus? Write your thoughts below:

....
....
....
....
....
....
....
....
....
....

Lord, bless my friendships.

The Transfiguration
Jesus is revealed as God the Son (Matthew 17 1-9)

After six days Jesus took Peter, James, and John his brother, and led them up a high mountain by themselves. And he was transfigured before them; his face shone like the sun and his clothes became white as light. And behold, Moses and Elijah appeared to them, conversing with him. Then Peter said to Jesus in reply, "Lord, it is good that we are here. If you wish, I will make three tents here, one for you, one for Moses, and one for Elijah." While he was still speaking, behold, a bright cloud cast a shadow over them. From the cloud came a voice that said, "This is my beloved Son, with whom I am well pleased; listen to him." When the disciples heard this, they fell prostrate and were very much afraid. But Jesus came and touched them, saying, "Rise, and do not be afraid." And when the disciples raised their eyes, they saw no one else but Jesus alone.

The Transfiguration gave Peter, James and John a glimpse of Jesus in all his glory, a foretaste of the fullness of God's Kingdom. We may not have been atop the mountain with the disciples, but we can experience transfiguration in our lives. God breaks through our every day to reveal his glory and remind us of His promises, we just need the eyes to see Him. This may be in the form of something miraculous happening in our life, or simply as a meaningful answer to a prayer. Spend some time reflecting on the ways God reveals Himself to you:

....
....
....
....
....
....
....
....
....
....
....

Open my eyes, Lord. Help me to see.

Institution of the Eucharist

Jesus established the Sacrament of the Eucharist (Mt 26:26-28)

While they were eating, Jesus took bread, said the blessing, broke it, and giving it to his disciples said, "Take and eat; this is my body." Then he took a cup, gave thanks, and gave it to them, saying, "Drink from it, all of you, for this is my blood of the covenant, which will be shed on behalf of many for the forgiveness of sins."

Take a moment to think of a mother breastfeeding her newborn baby. This child has just broken through the waters of her womb, and her body provides the nourishment required for growth and development. She continues to give of herself so that her child may have life. In a similar vein, after leaving the waters of Baptism, we are nourished by Jesus in the Eucharist. He gives his body so that we may have life, and have it to the full. Reflect on the areas in your life that you need Jesus to sustain you and help you grow:

....
....
....
....
....
....
....
....
....
....
....
....
....

Lord, increase in me.

Sorrowful Mysteries

The Agony in the Garden
Jesus prayed in the Garden of Gethsemane (Lk 22:41-44)

Jesus withdrew from his disciples, about a stone's throw away, and knelt down and prayed. "Father," he said, "if you are willing, take this cup away from me. Nevertheless, let your will be done, not mine." Then an angel appeared to him, coming from heaven to give him strength. In his anguish he prayed even more earnestly, and his sweat fell to the ground like great drops of blood.

"May your will be done"... Difficult words to utter when we are experiencing heartbreak, disappointment, anger, or simply when we desire to feel in 'control'. Yet, we are challenged by this Mystery to surrender ourselves to God and seek His will above all else, no matter what that entails. Use this space to write about something you feel is God's will, but are finding hard to do:

....
....
....
....
....
....
....
....
....
....
....
....
....
....

Lord, I surrender. May your will be done.

Scourging at the Pillar.
Jesus is whipped by soldiers (Jn 19:1)

Pilate had Jesus taken away and scourged.

A short passage, easily missed. Yet, it poignantly reminds us of Christ's suffering. Jesus did not shy away from the mess or chaos of pain, he lived through it for a greater purpose. This Mystery challenges us to consider whether we have veered from God's path for us in order to avoid suffering. This could be in many forms: turning a blind eye to wrongdoing for fear of exclusion, not speaking up to avoid upsetting someone. Use the space below to write about something you need strength or courage to do, and ask Jesus to give you the grace you need:

....
....
....
....
....
....
....
....
....
....
....
....
....

Lord, I choose your will. Grant me the grace I need.

The Crowning with Thorns
A crown of thorns is placed on Jesus (Jn 19: 2-3)

The soldiers twisted some thorns into a crown and put it on his head and dressed him in a purple robe. They kept coming up to him and saying, "Hail, king of the Jews!" and slapping him in the face. Pilate had Jesus taken away and scourged.

Christ, the King of Kings, deserved a golden crown. Instead, one of no value was placed upon him. This Mystery challenges us to consider the counterfeit crowns we place on Jesus. These come in many forms: empty religious practice, distracted prayer, prideful actions... anything that does not honor Jesus as it should. Does this make you think of anything in your life? Write about it in the space below:

....
....
....
....
....
....
....
....
....
....
....
....
....
....

Forgive me, Lord.

The Carrying of the Cross
Jesus carries His cross to be crucified (Jn 19:17-18)

They took charge of Jesus, and carrying his own cross he went out to the Place of the Skull or, as it is called in Hebrew, Golgotha, where they crucified him.

Jesus climbed to Golgotha with full knowledge of his fate. Despite this, he embraced his cross because he knew it was the tool for salvation. This Mystery challenges us to consider the crosses we have been asked to bear, and ponder how we might 'embrace' them. For example, we may need to endure physical pain with grace, forgive a person who treats us harshly, or give up a comfort for a greater good. Use the space below to write about the crosses in your life and how you may be called to carry them:

....
....
....
....
....
....
....
....
....
....
....
....
....
....

Jesus, give me strength to embrace my crosses.

Crucifixion and Death of our Lord.
Jesus dies on the cross (Jn 19:26-27, 30)

Seeing his mother and the disciple whom he loved standing near her, Jesus said to his mother, "Woman, this is your son." Then to the disciple he said, "This is your mother."... Jesus said, 'It is fulfilled'; and bowing his head he gave up his spirit.

Our Lady remained close to Jesus as he suffered, despite the sorrow this inflicted upon her. In the end, after Jesus was abandoned by his friends, it was she who was at the foot of the cross. In the same way, Mother Mary remains close to us when we suffer and, since she is never far from her Son, she connects us to Jesus. Use the space below to list the petitions you would like Mary to take to Jesus:

....
....
....
....
....
....
....
....
....
....
....
....
....
....
....
....

Mother Mary, intercede for me.

Glorious Mysteries

The Resurrection

Jesus rises from the dead three days after His crucifixion (Mt 28:1-8)

After the Sabbath, as the first day of the week was dawning, Mary Magdalene and another Mary came to see the tomb. And behold, there was a great earthquake; for an angel of the Lord descended from heaven, approached, rolled back the stone, and sat upon it. His appearance was like lightning and his clothing was white as snow. The guards were shaken with fear of him and became like dead men. Then the angel said to the women, "Do not be afraid! I know that you are seeking Jesus the crucified. He is not here, for he has been raised just as he said. Come and see the place where he lay. Then go quickly and tell his disciples, 'He has been raised from the dead, and he is going before you to Galilee; there you will see him.' Behold, I have told you." Then they went away quickly from the tomb, fearful yet overjoyed, and ran to announce this to his disciples.

The Resurrection is not simply an historical event, it is a reality. Christ is risen, He is alive. We can rattle off this belief when we say the creed, but what in our life speaks to this truth? Is it pondered in our hearts and minds? Do we run to share this good news with others? Use this space to write your reflections:

....
....
....
....
....
....
....
....
....
....
....

Christ is risen! Alleluia!

The Ascension
Forty days after rising from the dead, Jesus ascends into Heaven (Acts 1:8-11)

Jesus said to them: "You will receive power when the Holy Spirit comes upon you, and you will be my witnesses in Jerusalem, throughout Judea and Samaria, and to the ends of the earth." When he had said this, as they were looking on, he was lifted up, and a cloud took him from their sight. While they were looking intently at the sky as he was going, suddenly two men dressed in white garments stood beside them. They said, "Men of Galilee, why are you standing there looking at the sky? This Jesus who has been taken up from you into heaven will return in the same way as you have seen him going into heaven."

The power of the Holy Spirit is the grace to do what we ourselves cannot. This doesn't only apply to external works and ministries but, importantly, starts within. Perhaps we must challenge lies we have accepted about our self, or vices we cannot seem to overcome. Maybe our hearts need to reflect the charity of our words. True transformation can only occur by the grace of God, the power of the Holy Spirit. Reflect on how this might apply to you and your life:

....
....
....
....
....
....
....
....
....
....
....

Come, Holy Spirit. Work in me.

The Descent of the Holy Spirit

The Holy Spirit descends on Mary and the Apostles (Acts 2:1-6, 38-41)

When the time for Pentecost was fulfilled, they were all in one place together. And suddenly there came from the sky a noise like a strong driving wind, and it filled the entire house in which they were. Then there appeared to them tongues as of fire, which parted and came to rest on each one of them. And they were all filled with the Holy Spirit and began to speak in different tongues, as the Spirit enabled them to proclaim. Now there were devout Jews from every nation under heaven staying in Jerusalem. At this sound, they gathered in a large crowd, but they were confused because each one heard them speaking in his own language. Peter said to them, "Repent and be baptized, every one of you, in the name of Jesus Christ, for the forgiveness of your sins; and you will receive the gift of the Holy Spirit.

We receive the Holy Spirit as the disciples did by inviting Him to rain down upon us. And while we may not necessarily speak in 'different tongues', the language of our actions can be transformed in to proclamations of the Good News and bear witness to the world. Do you invite the Holy Spirit to work in and through you? What aspect of your life can you be a better witness to Christ's love? Write your thoughts in the space below:

....
....
....
....
....
....
....
....
....
....

Come, Holy Spirit. Work through me.

The Assumption of Mary
Mary is taken to Heaven, body and soul (Revelation 12:1, 13-14)

A great sign appeared in the sky, a woman clothed with the sun, with the moon under her feet, and on her head a crown of twelve stars. ... When the dragon saw that it had been thrown down to the earth, it pursued the woman who had given birth to the male child. But the woman was given two wings of the great eagle so that she could fly to her place in the desert, where, far from the serpent, she was taken care of.

Mary is taken up to heaven both "body and soul." Our Blessed Mother understood both the dignity and holiness of her body. The body was never an obstacle for her, but rather the means through which she glorified God and allowed His will to be done. Do we see our bodies in this way, or as an obstacle to our holiness and salvation? Do we ever thank God for our bodies, or do we simply critique them? Use this space to acknowledge the goodness of your body and what it has helped you achieve for the glory of God:

....
....
....
....
....
....
....
....
....
....
....
....

May I model myself after Mary.

The Coronation of Our Lady
Mary is crowned queen of Heaven and Earth (Revelation 12:1-3, 4-5)

A great sign appeared in the sky, a woman clothed with the sun, with the moon under her feet, and on her head a crown of twelve stars. She was with child and wailed aloud in pain as she labored to give birth. Then another sign appeared in the sky; it was a huge red dragon, with seven heads and ten horns, and on its heads were seven diadems. She gave birth to a son, a male child, destined to rule all the nations with an iron rod.

Honoring Mary does not detract from Christ. Since Mary is the perfect instrument of God's grace, we honor Christ through her. There are many ways that the Church as an institution honors Mary, but how do you do so in your life? In what ways can you honor her more lovingly?

....
....
....
....
....
....
....
....
....
....
....
....
....
....
....

Hail, Holy Queen.

Further Resources

This journal has been developed as part of a larger project which hopes to draw people to Christ through the Holy Rosary. Check out the official site where you will find a range of free resources intended for personal, parish and classroom use.

Ad Jesum Per Mariam

THE ROSARY PROJECT

www.therosaryproject.net

www.ingramcontent.com/pod-product-compliance
Lightning Source LLC
LaVergne TN
LVHW072023060526
838200LV00058B/4660